The LIGHT and the GLORY

Children's Activity Book

Ages 5–8

Peter J. Marshall   David Manuel Jr.

Designed by Paraclete Press

Fleming H. Revell
A Division of Baker Book House
Grand Rapids, Michigan 49516

"We love the children's version of **The Light and the Glory,** but isn't there something for even younger kids? Something to get them started?" We heard this so often, we decided to prepare this activity book. With the help of Anna Fishel, who did such a commendable job on the children's version, and artist Roger Snure, it is designed to introduce young Americans to the role God played in the founding and growth of this country. His role was well understood by young Pilgrim and Puritan children; indeed, until this century it was one of the first things all children learned as part of their national heritage. But in today's public elementary school system, it is virtually ignored.

We have included some activities too easy for eight-year-olds and some too hard for five-year-olds. A few ideas in the story line may need a parent's amplification, but all ages should enjoy coloring the pictures. Throughout, we have been guided by the principle that no child is too young to understand why we sing "God Bless America" and say "one nation under God" in the Pledge of Allegiance.

Peter Marshall
David Manuel

Fifth printing, April 1999

Printed and published in the United States of America

ISBN 0-8007-5574-X

For current information about all releases from Baker Book House, visit our web site:
http://www.bakerbooks.com

As a young mapmaker in the 15th century, Christopher Columbus felt God calling him to sail west to tell people about Jesus. Others were trying to reach the Indies, the islands of the Orient discovered by Marco Polo. They were trying to sail east, around Africa. Until Columbus, no one had ever dared to reach the Orient by sailing west.

An expedition to the Indies would be very expensive, and Columbus had no money. He went to Ferdinand and Isabella, the King and Queen of Spain, to ask for help. They agreed to give him three ships.

"Christo-ferens"
The name Christopher comes from the Latin, **Christo-ferens**, which means Christ-bearer.

How many three- and four-letter words can you make out of
COLUMBUS?

—— —— —— ——   —— —— —— ——

—— —— —— ——   —— —— —— ——

—— —— —— ——   —— —— —— ——

—— —— —— ——   —— —— —— ——

—— —— —— ——   —— —— —— ——

—— —— —— ——   —— —— —— ——

Answers on page 70

In the summer of 1492, Columbus set sail aboard the Santa Maria, with the Niña and the Pinta. He thought it would take a month to reach the Indies, but he reached the New World instead.

The sailors with Columbus were afraid. No one had ever gone so far west. They wanted him to turn around. Help Columbus sail the **Niña,** the **Pinta,** and the **Santa Maria** to the New World—and don't turn back when your crew becomes scared!

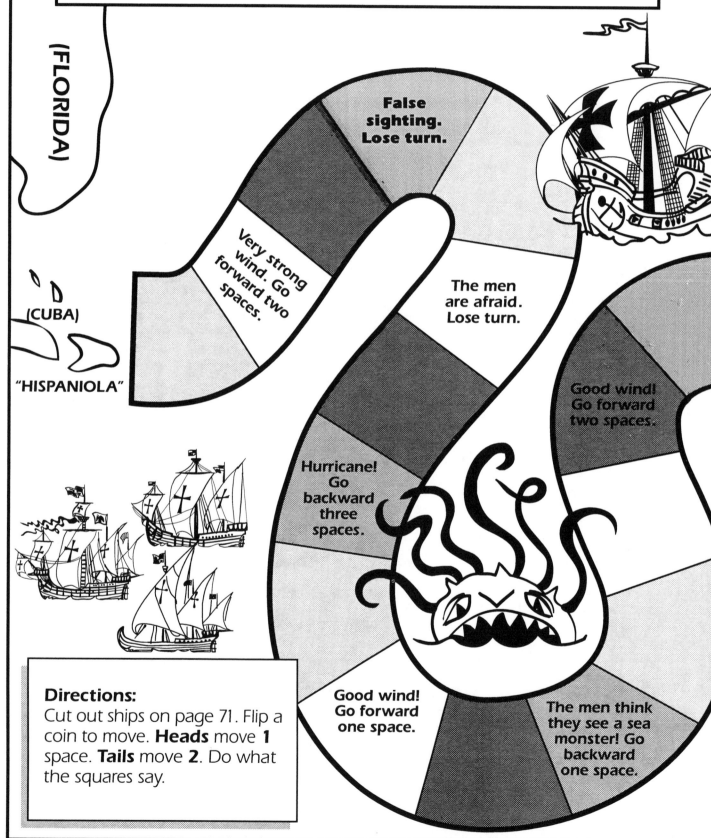

(FLORIDA)

(CUBA)

"HISPANIOLA"

False sighting. Lose turn.

Very strong wind. Go forward two spaces.

The men are afraid. Lose turn.

Good wind! Go forward two spaces.

Hurricane! Go backward three spaces.

Good wind! Go forward one space.

The men think they see a sea monster! Go backward one space.

Directions:
Cut out ships on page 71. Flip a coin to move. **Heads** move **1** space. **Tails** move **2**. Do what the squares say.

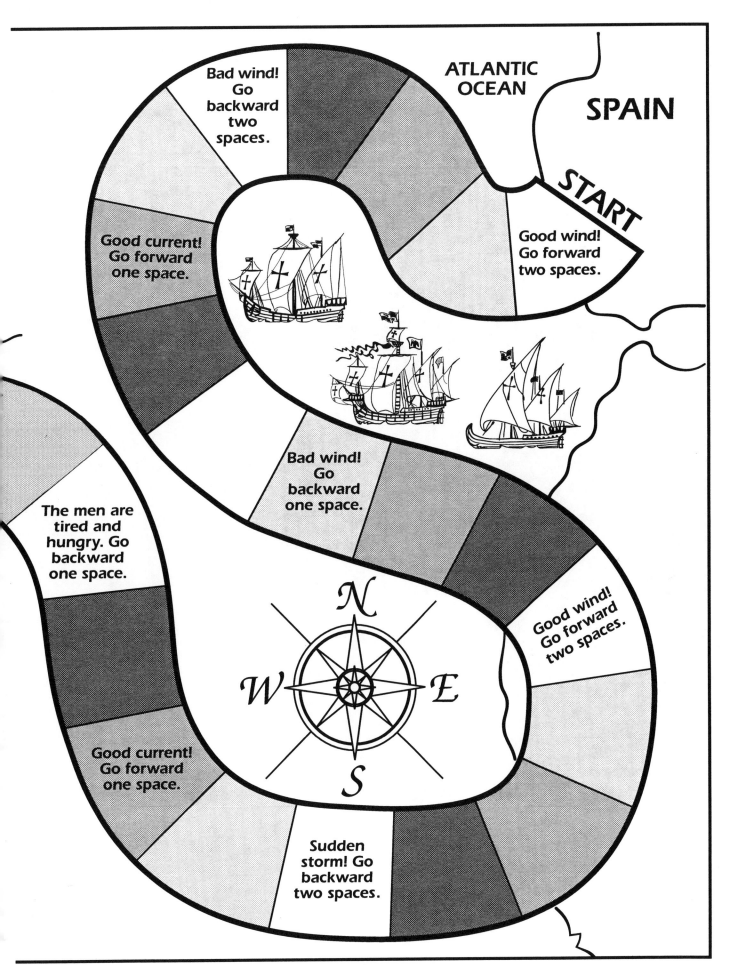

ATLANTIC OCEAN

SPAIN

START

Good wind! Go forward two spaces.

Bad wind! Go backward two spaces.

Good current! Go forward one space.

Bad wind! Go backward one space.

The men are tired and hungry. Go backward one space.

Good wind! Go forward two spaces.

Good current! Go forward one space.

Sudden storm! Go backward two spaces.

N

W *E*

S

When they finally found land, the first thing Columbus did was to give thanks to God. He named the island **San Salvador**, which means "Holy Savior." And because he thought he had reached the Indies, he called the people who lived there "Indians."

Columbus was soon followed by other explorers. Missionaries came with them to tell the Indians about Jesus. Their missions in the Southwest of the New World were named after saints.

San Francisco
San Jose
Santa Cruz
CALIFORNIA
Santa Maria
Santa Barbara
Santa Monica
Los Angeles
Santa Ana
San Diego

Other missionaries came to the northeastern part of the New World. All learned the language of the Indian tribe they lived with, so that they could tell them about Jesus. In this way, a number of Indians came to know and love the Lord.

When we write something, we use letters to make words. The Indians wrote by drawing pictures. Here is an Indian message. It was written by Indians who love Jesus. Can you decode it?

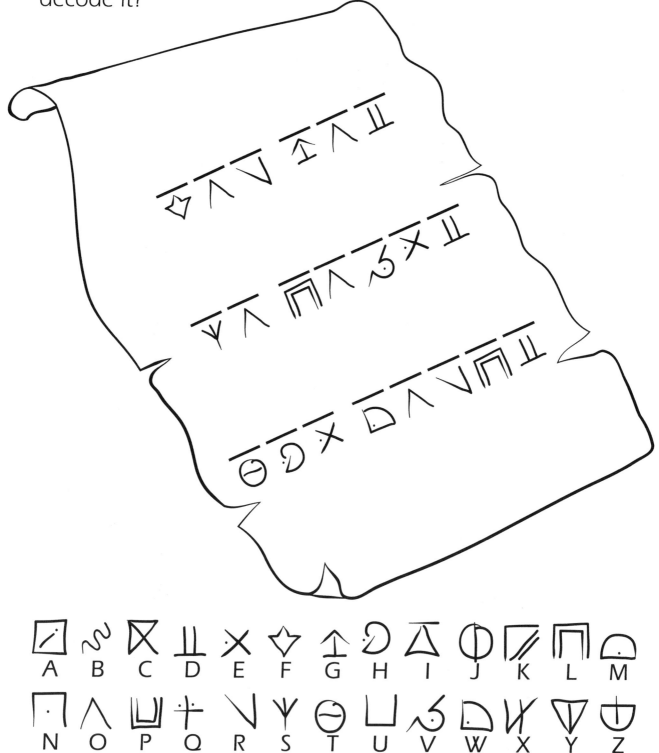

Do you know the rest of John 3:16? (You may have to ask Mom or Dad.)

Answer on page 70

One of the missionaries to the New World was Father Jacques Marquette. He was the first European to go down the Mississippi.

The missionaries found many different tribes of Indians in the New World. How many can you find below?

```
B  R  T  U  K  M  D  J  E  W  C  A
F  T  P  L  H  N  V  A  Z  B  H  N
I  R  O  Q  U  O  I  S  A  X  I  T
A  W  D  M  G  W  I  H  R  U  P  W
H  E  V  O  R  O  K  U  Q  S  P  G
U  F  R  J  N  X  W  N  H  L  E  R
R  T  S  I  M  D  O  Z  J  A  W  T
O  M  L  B  P  G  V  B  R  C  A  K
N  L  U  W  L  E  C  Y  Q  I  D  L
I  X  Q  A  T  M  J  L  B  W  P  Z
R  U  V  Z  I  F  H  D  O  N  G  Y
```

Word Bank
IROQUOIS
HURON
ALGONQUIN
ILLINOIS
CHIPPEWA
OJIBWA

Answers on page 70

In 1607, English settlers arrived in the New World. They set up the colony of Jamestown in the territory known as Virginia.

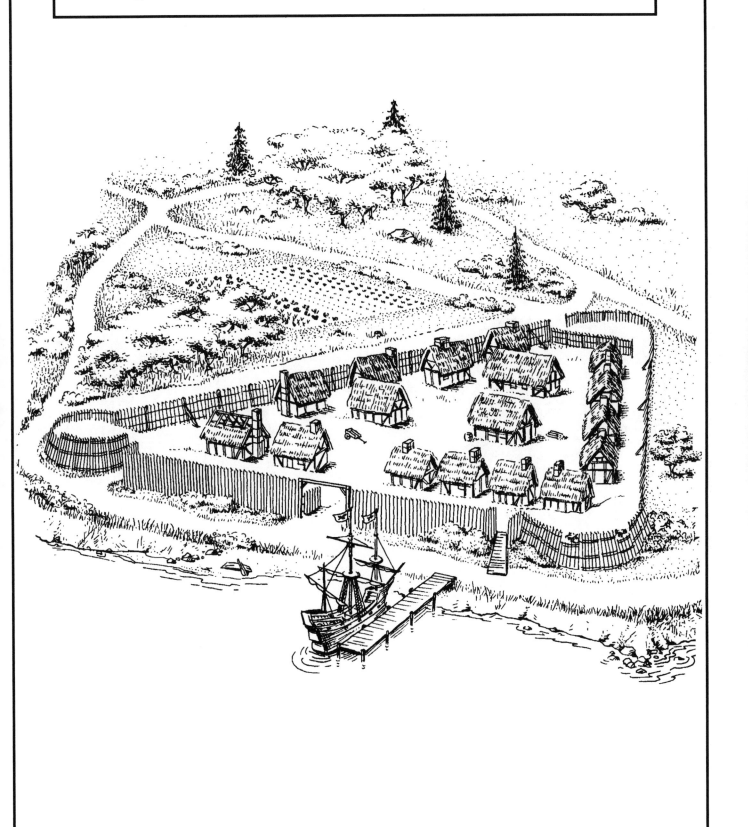

The Reverend Robert Hunt came with the Jamestown colonists to tell the Indians about Jesus. His first worship service, which was held under a sail, was for the settlers. Most of them did not listen.

The settlers at Jamestown were more interested in finding gold and pearls than in being obedient to God. They did not plant corn or wheat, and so, later, many went hungry and died. In this maze, find the path that leads to God.

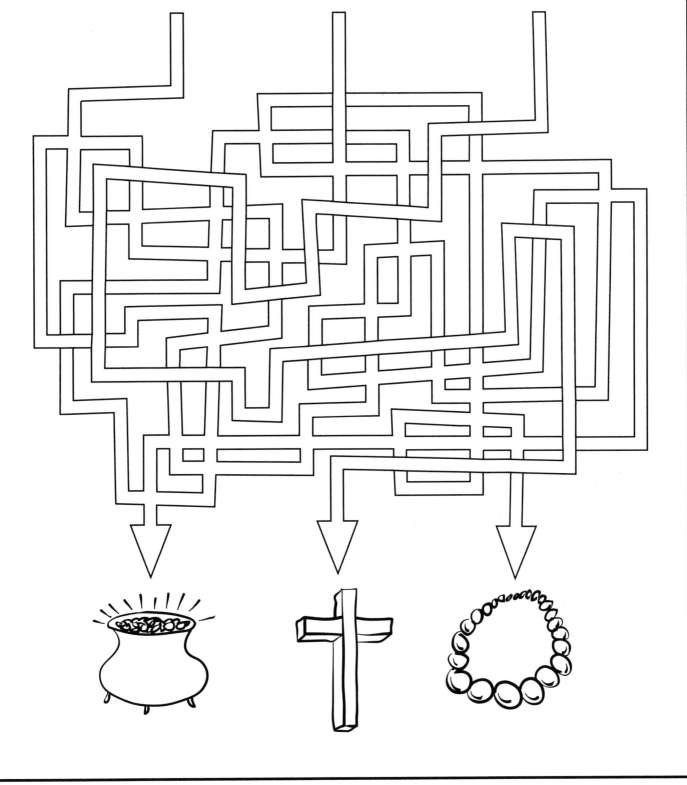

The Pilgrims were a group of English people who loved Jesus. They obeyed His call to come to America to tell the Indians about God and live there for Him.

What were the most important values in the Pilgrims' lives?

Word Bank

Liberty
Providence
Hope
Charity
Law
Faith
Education
Obedience
Wisdom

ACROSS

1. God wants us to obey His _____.
2. The Bible talks about faith, _____, and love.
4. An old word for God's care for us.
7. An old word for love.
8. "The fear of the Lord is the beginning of _____."

DOWN

1. Another word for freedom.
3. When parents tell children to do something, they expect _____.
5. "_____, hope, and love."
6. We go to school to get an _____.

Answers on page 70

If you were going on the Mayflower to the New World, what things would you take?

When the Pilgrims sailed away on the Mayflower, they left behind their homes, their families, and their friends. All they had now was each other and God.

Cross section of the Mayflower. The biggest thing the Pilgrims brought with them was Elder William Brewster's printing press. Find the press and circle the things the Pilgrims would **not** have brought.

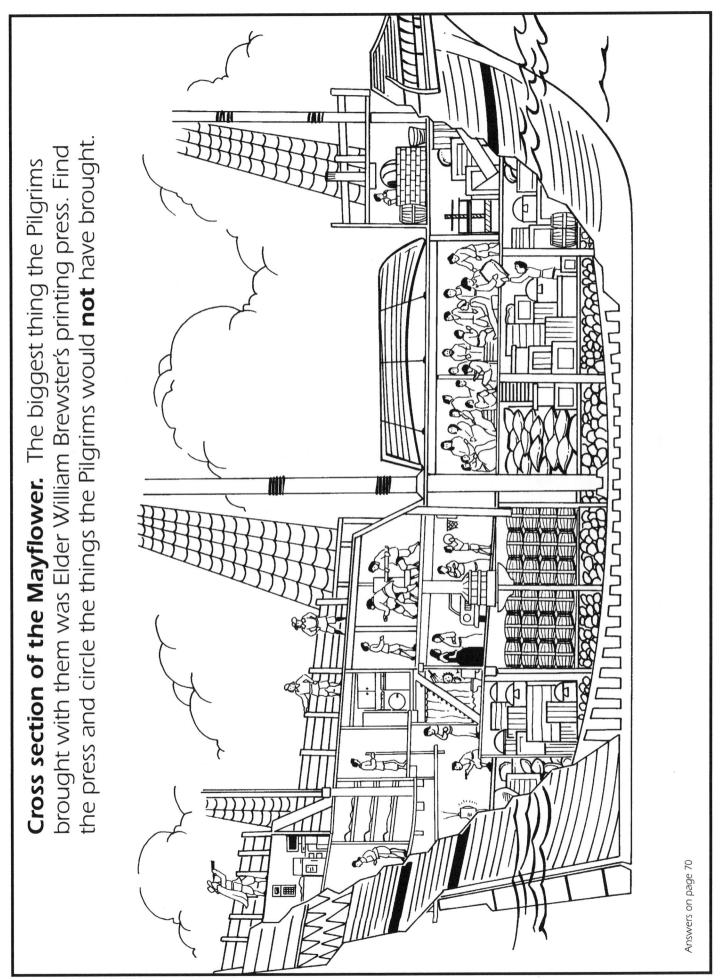

Answers on page 70

When the Pilgrims reached the New World, they anchored inside the tip of Cape Cod. Then God led them in a boat around the inside of the Cape, to where He wanted them to live. Help them find their way to Plymouth.

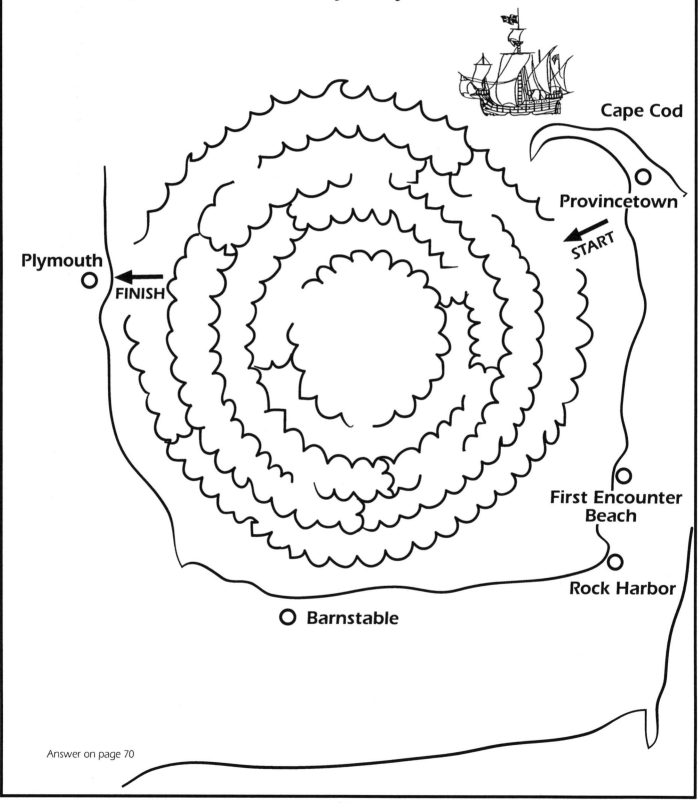

Cape Cod

Provincetown

START

Plymouth

FINISH

First Encounter Beach

Rock Harbor

O Barnstable

Answer on page 70

Each year the Pilgrims asked God: "Who should be our governor?" Year after year, they elected William Bradford.

To make a home in the wilderness, the Pilgrims needed a few basic tools. Can you unscramble the words and match them to their picture?

oeh _ _ _

kicp _ _ _ _ _

xea _ _ _

asw _ _ _

depas _ _ _ _ _ _

tuskem _ _ _ _ _ _ _

larreb _ _ _ _ _ _ _

Answers on page 70

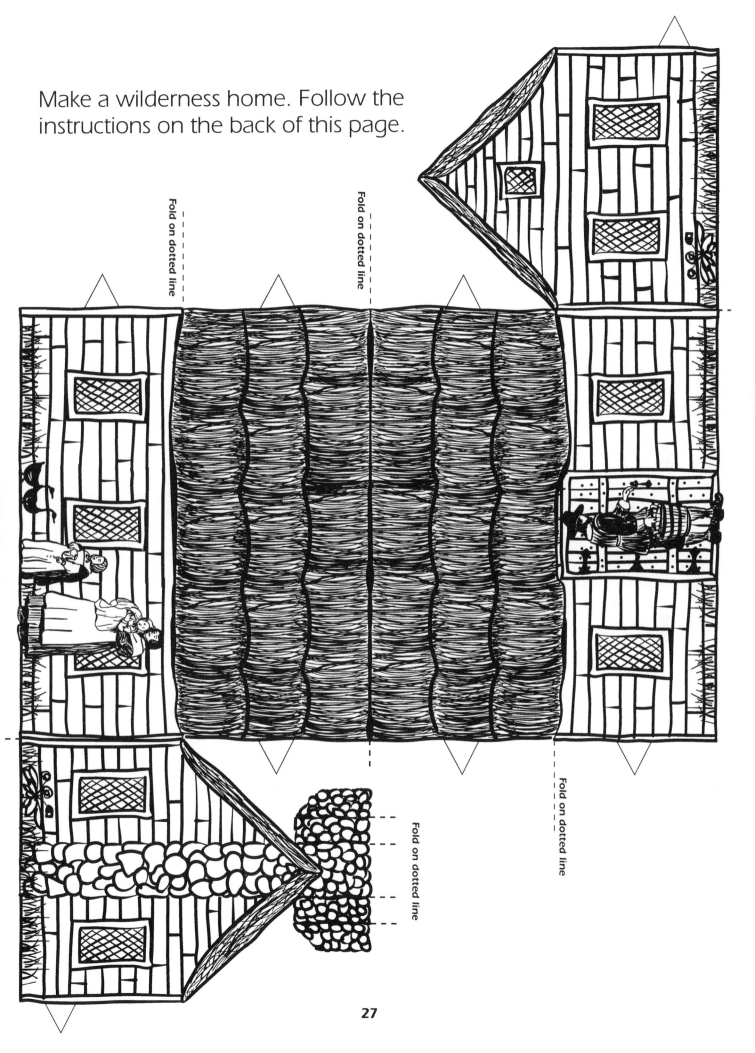

Make a wilderness home. Follow the instructions on the back of this page.

Fold on dotted line

Fold on dotted line

Fold on dotted line

Fold on dotted line

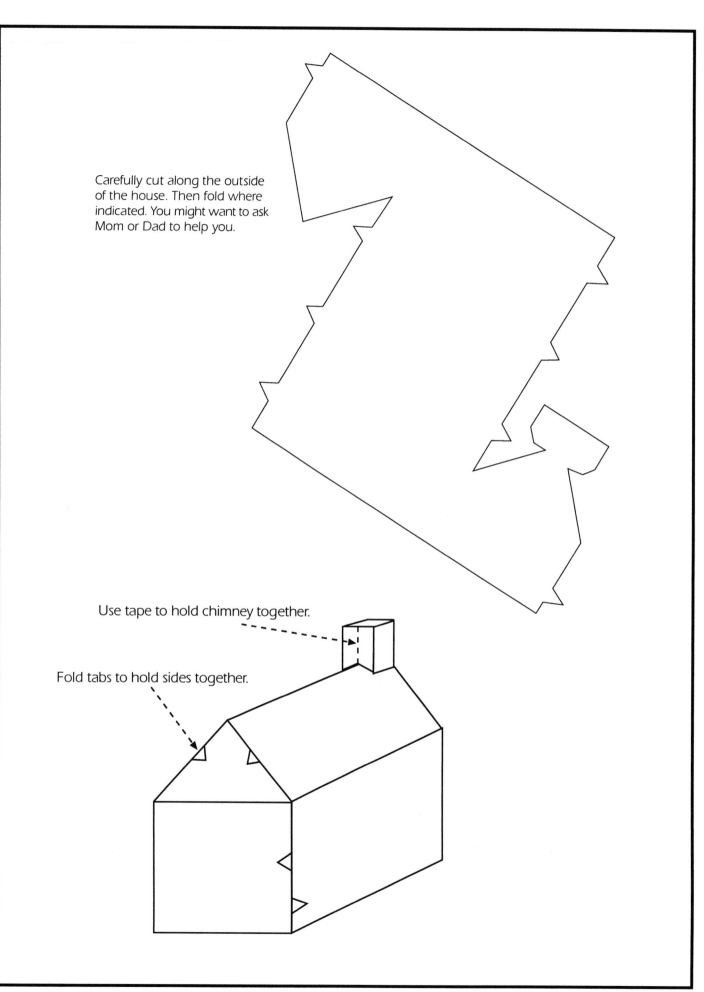

Carefully cut along the outside
of the house. Then fold where
indicated. You might want to ask
Mom or Dad to help you.

Use tape to hold chimney together.

Fold tabs to hold sides together.

The Pilgrims prayed and asked God to protect them from these dangers.

ACROSS

2. What makes the ground white in winter?
3. Sometimes the Pilgrims got so sick that they _____.
5. When you have to stay in bed and can't go outside, you have a _____.
7. What you feel when you haven't eaten in a long time.

DOWN

1. In the winter it is _____ outside.
4. Native Americans.
6. Hockey is played on _____.

Answers on page 70

By the end of the first winter, the Pilgrims were nearly out of food. Just in time, God sent them an Indian named Squanto. He taught them how to catch fish and plant corn.

Thanks to Squanto, they had many good things to eat.
Connect the dots to see what some of the things were.

The First Thanksgiving

After their harvest, the Pilgrims invited their Indian friends to join them in giving thanks to God.

Ten years after the Pilgrims came to Plymouth, the Puritans settled where Boston is now. Their leader was John Winthrop. He became their Governor.

The Pilgrims and Puritans had much in common. Can you find the hidden traits they shared?

```
A  Y  D  I  J  P  M  Q  X  R  S  E  W
Z  U  C  H  F  L  T  K  O  V  C  N  Y
V  O  R  C  O  V  E  N  A  N  T  D  O
T  B  D  G  P  L  M  S  A  F  J  P  B
E  S  N  Z  O  Q  I  T  U  L  H  Z  E
K  U  V  H  C  Y  N  N  X  C  O  B  D
J  X  C  I  T  E  L  V  E  D  N  F  I
D  A  O  G  P  W  O  R  K  S  E  G  E
L  B  U  E  H  R  I  U  M  H  S  A  N
M  O  R  O  F  S  A  B  Z  D  T  R  C
V  F  A  I  T  H  D  Y  U  W  Y  L  E
U  N  G  S  R  C  P  W  E  K  H  B  F
Z  D  E  J  L  X  O  M  E  R  C  Y  A
```

Word Bank
FAITH
REPENTANCE
HOLINESS
WORK
COURAGE
HONESTY
PRAYER
MERCY
COVENANT
OBEDIENCE

Answers on page 70

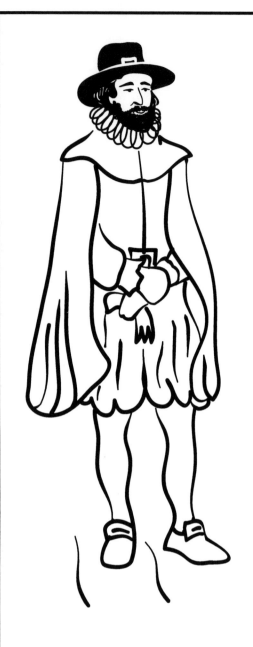

The Puritans had to work very hard. Everyone did what he or she was asked to do. Many did things they had never done before. What tasks would Governor Winthrop **not** have assigned?

clearing fields

catching fish

playing tennis

planting corn

building a dock

washing the car

chopping firewood

going to the mall

building a school

watching television

Whenever the Puritans started a new town in the wilderness, they put the church in the center because God was at the center of their lives.

Cut out the pictures on page 71 and build a Puritan town by pasting them where they fit below.

Working together is fun. The Puritans did all sorts of things as a group. Their older children joined in.

Can you unscramble the words to find out what they did?

LSELNIPG   _ _ _ _ _ _ _ _

GIWNSE   _ _ _ _ _ _

IGQTLNUI   _ _ _ _ _ _ _ _

NKOCGIO   _ _ _ _ _ _ _

SNGUHIK   _ _ _ _ _ _ _

SEUHO IRSGANI   _ _ _ _ _ - _ _ _ _ _ _

YPEARR   _ _ _ _ _ _

PISOWRH   _ _ _ _ _ _ _

Word Bank
QUILTING
PRAYER
HUSKING
WORSHIP
COOKING
SPELLING
HOUSE-RAISING
SEWING

Answers on page 70

Of all the things the Puritans did during the week, the most important was going to church.

In church they learned what was pleasing to God, and what was not. Can you unscramble the words and draw a line to their opposite?

DEBOCENIE   THEA

THIFA   MOLOG

YOJ   RWA

VOLE   TUBOD

FLIEBE   REAF

CEEPA   DSEBDOCENIIE

STRUT   LEBIUNFE

Word Bank
LOVE
HATE
TRUST
DOUBT
BELIEF
UNBELIEF
OBEDIENCE
DISOBEDIENCE
PEACE
WAR
FAITH
FEAR
JOY
GLOOM

Answers on page 70

Puritan children learned the alphabet with the help of these rhymes. Six names have been left blank. See if you can tell who they are.

In **A**_____'s Fall,
We sinned all.

Heaven to find,
The **B**_____ mind.

Christ crucified,
For sinners died.

The **D**eluge drowned
The Earth around.

Elijah hid,
By Ravens fed.

The Judgment made
Felix afraid.

As runs the **G**lass,
Our Life doth pass.

My Book and **H**eart
Must never part.

Job feels the Rod,
Yet blesses God.

Proud **K**arah's Troop,
Was swallowed up.

Lot fled to Zoar,
Saw fiery Shower
On Sodom pour.

M_____ was he
Who Israel's Host
Led through the Sea.

Noah did view
The old world and new.

Young **O**badias,
David, Josias,
All were pious.

P_____ denied
His Lord and cried.

Queen Esther sues,
And saves the Jews.

Young pious **R**_____,
Left all for Truth.

Young **S**amuel dear,
The Lord did fear.

Young **T**imothy
Learned Sin to fly.

Vashti for Pride,
Was set aside.

Whales in the Sea,
God's voice obey.

Xerxes did die,
And so must I.

While **Y**outh do cheer
Death may be near.

Z_____ he
Did climb the Tree,
Our Lord to see.

Answers on page 70

What were some of the things that Puritan children learned about the Christian faith?

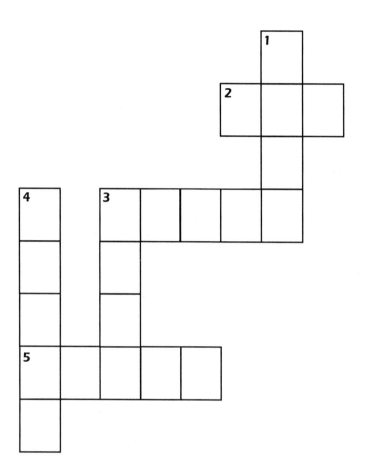

ACROSS

2. Our heavenly Father.
3. When Jesus was born, the angels said "_____ on earth."
5. Another word for faithful.

DOWN

1. God is _____.
3. To talk to God.
4. God's Word.

Answers on page 70

In the 18th century, America's most famous evangelist was George Whitefield. He rode on horseback to every Colony, telling people about Jesus. He preached that God created all men equal.

By 1763, there were 13 states. Can you draw a line to where they were?

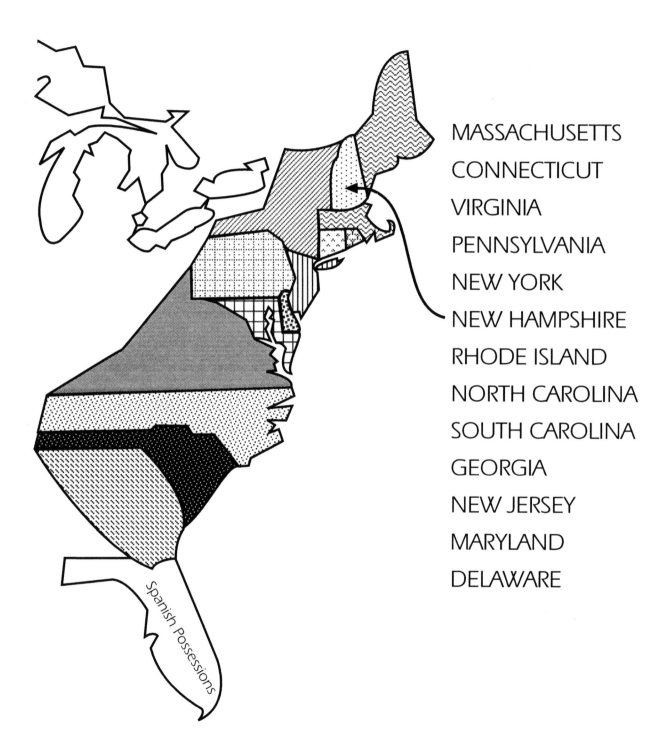

MASSACHUSETTS

CONNECTICUT

VIRGINIA

PENNSYLVANIA

NEW YORK

NEW HAMPSHIRE

RHODE ISLAND

NORTH CAROLINA

SOUTH CAROLINA

GEORGIA

NEW JERSEY

MARYLAND

DELAWARE

Spanish Possessions

Hint: One state claimed two areas.

Answers on page 70

Trade between America and Great Britain became important. Which goods did this ship carry to America? Which did it carry back to England?

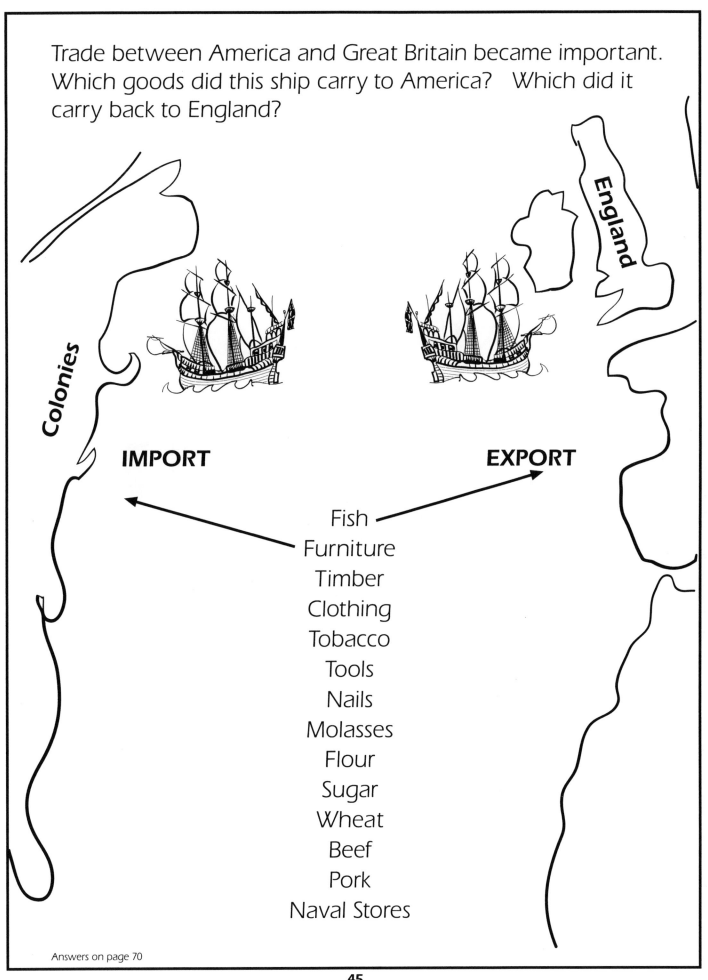

England

Colonies

IMPORT

EXPORT

Fish
Furniture
Timber
Clothing
Tobacco
Tools
Nails
Molasses
Flour
Sugar
Wheat
Beef
Pork
Naval Stores

Answers on page 70

King George of England wanted the Americans to pay unfair taxes. He put a tax on everything—even stamps, tea, and marriage licenses!

The Americans got angry. They dressed up as Indians and threw the British tea into Boston Harbor. They called it "The Boston Tea Party."

King George was very angry at the Americans. He sent many British soldiers to America, to make the colonists do what he wanted them to.

Circle the two soldiers who are exactly the same.

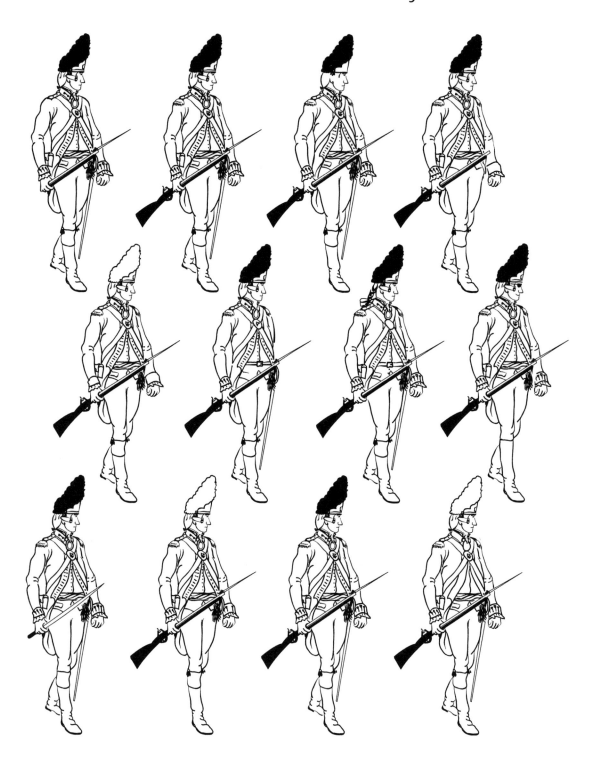

Answer on page 70

The Americans wanted to keep their freedom. To fool the British, they sent secret messages to each other. Can you decode this one?

$\overline{6}\ \overline{2}\qquad \overline{19}\ \overline{17}\ \overline{6}\ \overline{25}$

$\overline{15}\ \overline{22}\ \overline{3}\qquad \overline{19}\ \overline{17}\ \overline{6}\ \overline{25}$

$\overline{10}\ \overline{5}\ \overline{11}\ \overline{22}\ \overline{11}$

1	2	3	4	5	6	7	8	9	10	11	12	13
R	O	T	W	E	N	Y	H	Q	J	S	L	Z

14	15	16	17	18	19	20	21	22	23	24	25	26
F	B	P	I	A	K	C	V	U	D	X	G	M

Answer on page 70

The British soldiers wore red coats with crossed white belts. The Americans, who were ready to defend their homes in a minute, had no uniforms.

MINUTEMAN   REDCOAT

On April 18, 1775, Paul Revere rode through the night, warning everyone: "The British are coming!" The British Redcoats marched out of Boston and headed for Concord.

At Lexington, the Minutemen ran to the village green to stop the British.

Fill in the missing letters in each Founding Father's name, then put the letters in the blanks below, above their numbers, and finish what Samuel Adams said.

S__MUEL ADAMS   J__HN JAY
  1   11

THO__AS JEFF__RSON   JOHN HAN__OC__
  2   3   12   13

PATR__CK HENR__   JOHN WITHERSPO__N
  4   5   14

JOHN A__AMS   JOHN RA__DOLPH
        6   15

GEOR__E WAS__INGTON   JAMES __ADI__ON
  7   8   16   17

BENJA__IN FRANKL__N
  9   10

"We have this day restored the Sovereign, to whom alone men ought to be obedient. He reigns in heaven, and from the rising to the setting sun . . ."

$\overline{}\ \overline{}\ \overline{}\quad \overline{}\ \overline{}\ \overline{}\quad \overline{}\ \overline{}\ \overline{}\ \overline{}\ \overline{}\ \overline{}\ \overline{}\quad \overline{}\ \overline{}\ \overline{}\ \overline{}$
 9 1 5   8 4 17   13 10 15 7 6 11 2   12 14 16 3

Samuel Adams
August 2, 1776

Ask your Mom or Dad who these great men were.

Answers on page 70

At the old North Bridge in Concord, the Minutemen fought the British and made them retreat to Boston.

How many three- or four-letter words can you find in the last
name of the American army's Commander-in-Chief, GEORGE

WASHINGTON

___ ___ ___ ___   ___ ___ ___ ___

___ ___ ___ ___   ___ ___ ___ ___

___ ___ ___ ___   ___ ___ ___ ___

___ ___ ___ ___   ___ ___ ___ ___

___ ___ ___ ___   ___ ___ ___ ___

___ ___ ___ ___   ___ ___ ___ ___

___ ___ ___ ___   ___ ___ ___ ___

Answers on page 70

The Signing of the Declaration of Independence

On the Fourth of July, 1776, America declared herself a free republic, independent of Great Britain. We celebrate our nation's birthday every year!

When the British attacked New York City, the American army, under General Washington, left Boston and hurried to stop them at Brooklyn on Long Island. Can you help them find the way?

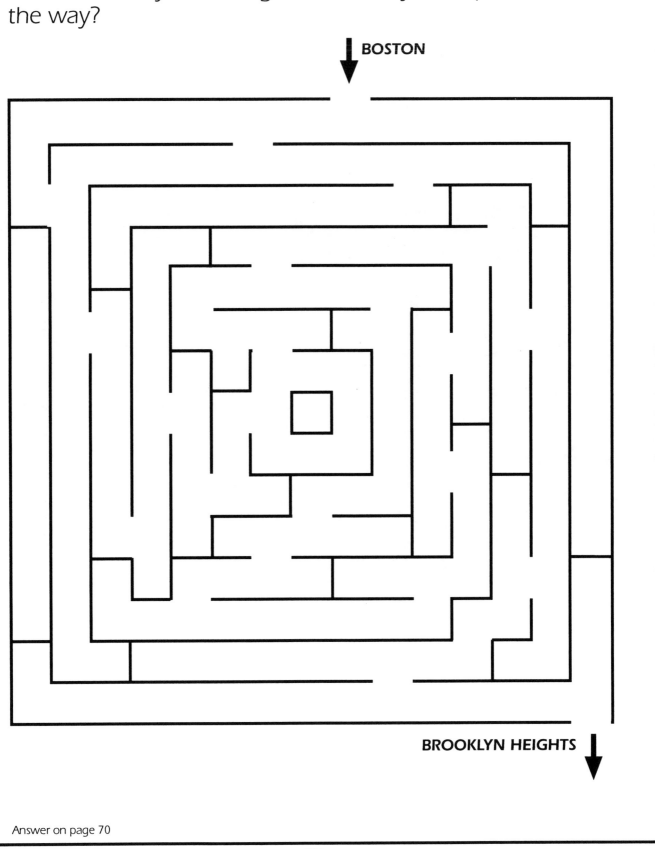

BOSTON

BROOKLYN HEIGHTS

Answer on page 70

After a fierce battle, the outnumbered Americans were surrounded on Brooklyn Heights. But God sent a fog to cover their escape to Manhattan. Not a soldier was lost!

The soldiers spent one winter in a place called Valley Forge. They did not have enough to eat or enough clothes to keep warm. Many grew very sick. But they never stopped praying.

Starting with the letter T, use every third letter to spell out the hidden message and write it in the blanks below.

Answer on page 70

_ _ _ _ _ _ _ _ _ _ _ _ _ _

As the leader of the American Army, George Washington knew how cold and hungry his men were, and how desperate their situation was. There was only one Person he could turn to for help. Often he would ride alone into the woods to pray.

The American army suffered terribly that winter in Valley Forge. Sometimes they wondered if they would win their struggle to be free. Can you help them find their way to freedom?

START

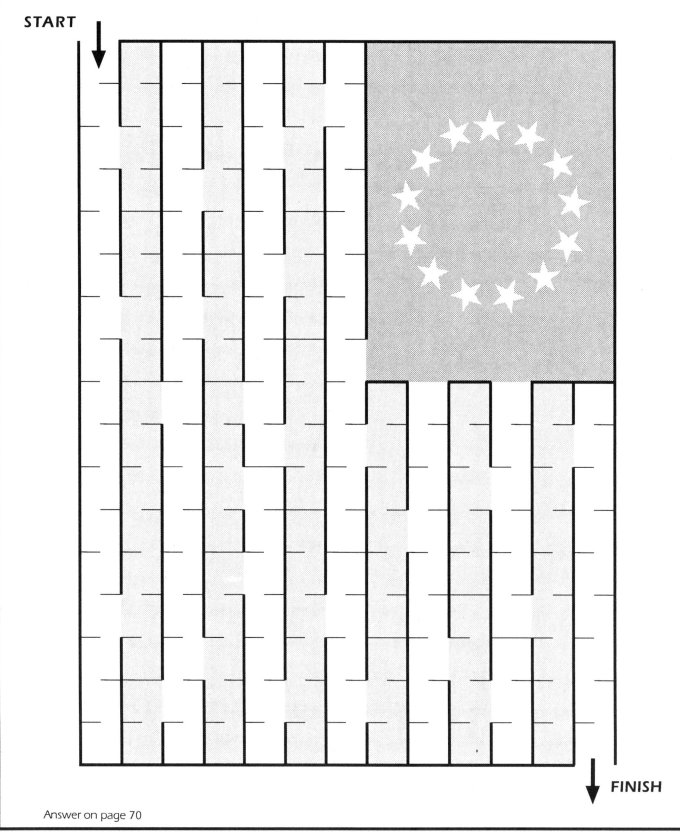

FINISH

Answer on page 70

The Surrender of Yorktown

After Valley Forge, the Americans never lost another battle. At Yorktown, Virginia, they won the one that decided the war.

The Americans had won their independence! To celebrate, they rang every church bell in the land. Now at last they were free to be . . .

$\overline{12}\ \overline{2}\ \overline{14}\quad \overline{11}\ \overline{6}\ \overline{13}\ \overline{16}\ \overline{17}\ \overline{4}\quad \overline{7}\ \overline{10}\ \overline{5}\ \overline{3}\ \overline{8}\quad \overline{9}\ \overline{15}\ \overline{1}$

IN__EPE__D__NCE
  1   2   3

U__ITE__ ST__TES
  4   5   6

Fill in the missing letters in these words. Then put the letters in the right spaces above to see the rest of the message.

REP__BLIC
   7

LIBE__TY
    8

SELF-__OVER__ME__T
      9   10   11

FREED__M
      12

JUS__IC__
   13   14

C__NST__TUTI__N
 15   16   17

Answer on page 70

"Let freedom ring throughout the land!" The Liberty Bell of Independence Hall in Philadelphia was first rung on July 8, 1776.

Connect the dots.

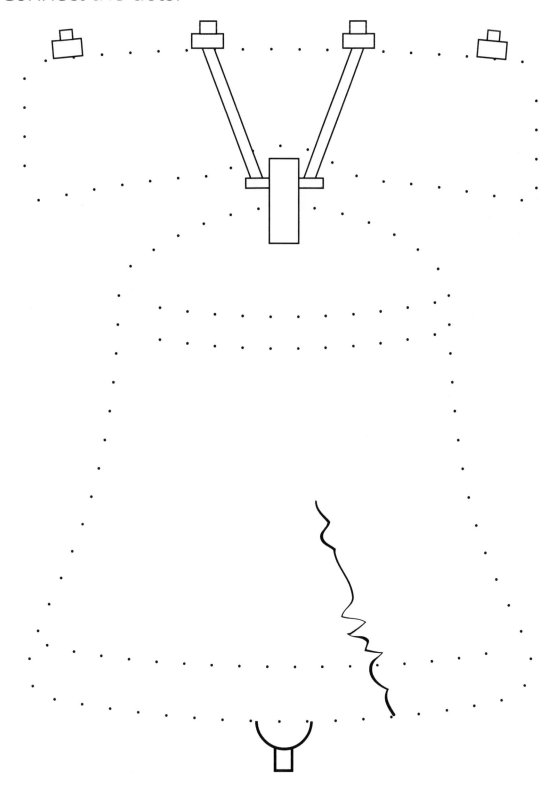

In 1787, the United States of America badly needed to create a Constitution. But the delegates wound up arguing – until Ben Franklin asked everyone to pray.

Our first President, George Washington, placed his hand on the Bible and took the oath of office, promising God that he would do his best.

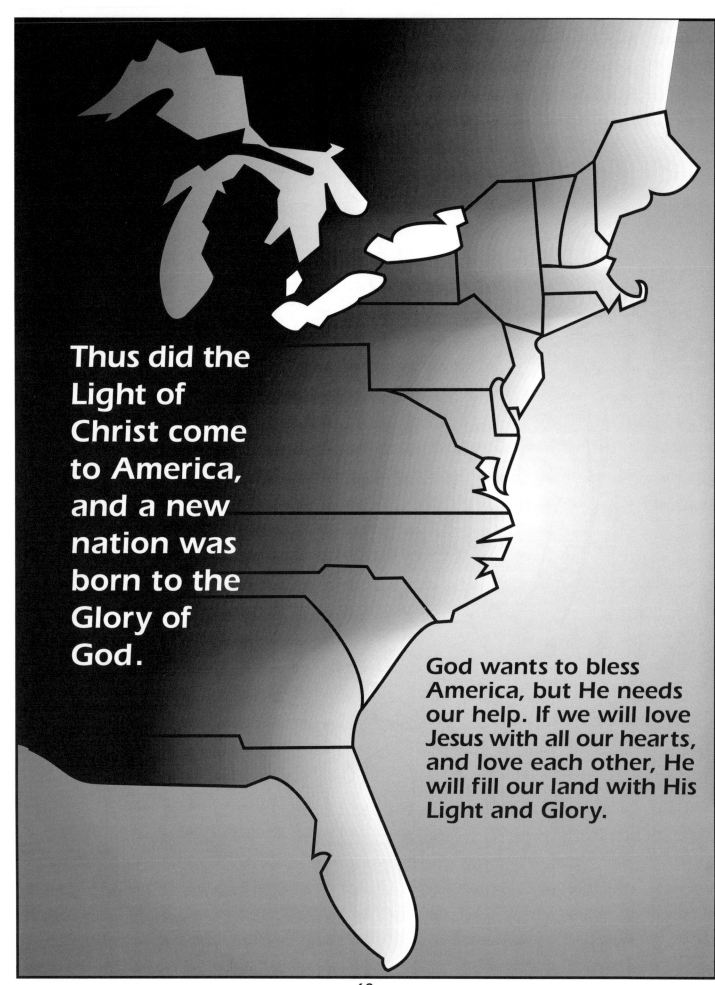

Thus did the Light of Christ come to America, and a new nation was born to the Glory of God.

God wants to bless America, but He needs our help. If we will love Jesus with all our hearts, and love each other, He will fill our land with His Light and Glory.

This is to certify that I,

_____

on the _____ *day of* _____

in the One thousand, nine hundred and

_____ *Year of our Lord,*

have completed this book.

_____
Signature

_____
Witness

ANSWERS

Page 6
COMB   MOB(S)
SCUM   COB(S)
SLUM   LOB(S)
CLUB   SOB
SLOB   BUS
SOUL   SUM

Page 14
For God so loved the world

Page 16

Page 20
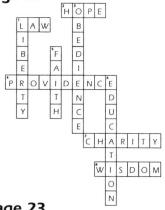

Page 23
Calendar   Television
Automobile   Washer/Dryer
Shower   Basketball
Wristwatch   Computer
Toilet   Refrigerator

Page 24
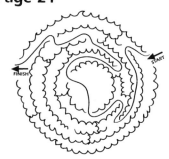

Page 26
Hoe   Pick
Axe   Saw
Spade   Musket
Barrel

Page 29

Page 35
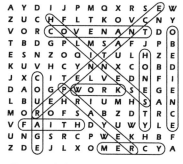

Page 38
SPELLING   SEWING
QUILTING   COOKING
HUSKING   HOUSE-RAISING
PRAYER   WORSHIP

Page 40
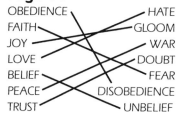

OBEDIENCE — HATE
FAITH — GLOOM
JOY — WAR
LOVE — DOUBT
BELIEF — FEAR
PEACE — DISOBEDIENCE
TRUST — UNBELIEF

Page 41
Adam   Bible
Moses   Peter
Ruth   Zaccheus

Page 42
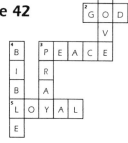

Page 45

IMPORT	EXPORT
Furniture	Fish
Clothing	Timber
Tools	Tobacco
Nails	Flour
Molasses	Wheat
Sugar	Beef
Naval Stores	Pork

Page 44
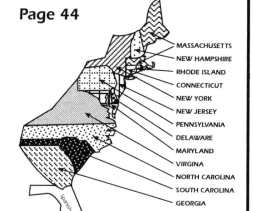

MASSACHUSETTS
NEW HAMPSHIRE
RHODE ISLAND
CONNECTICUT
NEW YORK
NEW JERSEY
PENNSYLVANIA
DELAWARE
MARYLAND
VIRGINA
NORTH CAROLINA
SOUTH CAROLINA
GEORGIA
Spanish Possessions

Page 48
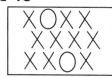

Page 49
NO KING BUT KING JESUS

Page 53
MAY HIS KINGDOM COME

Page 55
WASH   SHOT
TON   WAS
SING   HATS
WING   NOT

Page 57

BOSTON
BROOKLYN HEIGHTS

Page 59
TRUST IN GOD

Page 62
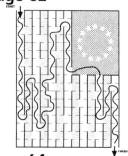
START
FINISH

Page 64
ONE NATION UNDER GOD

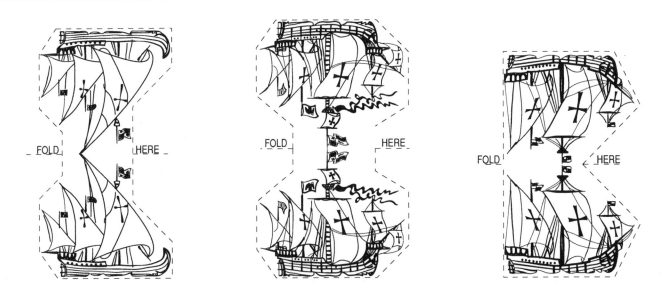

FOLD   HERE

FOLD   HERE

FOLD   HERE

Cut along dotted line to make playing pieces for pages 8 and 9.

Cut out the buildings for the Puritan town on page 37.